THE ACCIDENT LO(

MW00955058

HEALTH & SAFETY INCIDENT RECORD BOOK

COMPANY & LOG BOOK DETAILS			
Log Start Date:		**Log Book No.**	
Name:			
Address:			
Email:			
Telephone No.			
Emergency Contact:			

Published by
Accident Log & Incident Report Books Publishing

ACCIDENT / INCIDENT REPORT FORM

Incident Date:		*Reported by:*		*Report Date:*	
Incident Time:		*Location:*			

Person Involved /Injured:	Employee	Contractor	Visitor	General Public	Member	Other
Full Name:						
Address:						
Tel:			*Email:*			

DESCRIPTION OF ACCIDENT / INCIDENT

ACTION TAKEN / ACTIONS WHICH MAY PREVENT FUTURE REOCCURRENCE

WITNESS/ES

Full Name:		*Contact:*	
Full Name:		*Contact:*	
Full Name:		*Contact:*	
Form Completed by:		*Signed:*	
Approved by:		*Signed:*	

ACCIDENT / INCIDENT REPORT FORM

Incident Date:		*Reported by:*		*Report Date:*	
Incident Time:		*Location:*			

Person Involved /Injured:	Employee	Contractor	Visitor	General Public	Member	Other
Full Name:						
Address:						
Tel:			*Email:*			

DESCRIPTION OF ACCIDENT / INCIDENT

ACTION TAKEN / ACTIONS WHICH MAY PREVENT FUTURE REOCCURRENCE

WITNESS/ES

Full Name:		*Contact:*	
Full Name:		*Contact:*	
Full Name:		*Contact:*	
Form Completed by:		*Signed:*	
Approved by:		*Signed:*	

ACCIDENT / INCIDENT REPORT FORM

Incident Date:		*Reported by:*		*Report Date:*	
Incident Time:		*Location:*			

Person Involved /Injured:	Employee	Contractor	Visitor	General Public	Member	Other
Full Name:						
Address:						
Tel:			*Email:*			

DESCRIPTION OF ACCIDENT / INCIDENT

ACTION TAKEN / ACTIONS WHICH MAY PREVENT FUTURE REOCCURRENCE

WITNESS/ES

Full Name:		*Contact:*	
Full Name:		*Contact:*	
Full Name:		*Contact:*	
Form Completed by:		*Signed:*	
Approved by:		*Signed:*	

ACCIDENT / INCIDENT REPORT FORM

Incident Date:		*Reported by:*		*Report Date:*	
Incident Time:		*Location:*			

Person Involved /Injured:	Employee	Contractor	Visitor	General Public	Member	Other
Full Name:						
Address:						
Tel:			*Email:*			

DESCRIPTION OF ACCIDENT / INCIDENT

ACTION TAKEN / ACTIONS WHICH MAY PREVENT FUTURE REOCCURRENCE

WITNESS/ES

Full Name:		*Contact:*	
Full Name:		*Contact:*	
Full Name:		*Contact:*	
Form Completed by:		*Signed:*	
Approved by:		*Signed:*	

ACCIDENT / INCIDENT REPORT FORM

Incident Date:		*Reported by:*		*Report Date:*	
Incident Time:		*Location:*			

Person Involved /Injured:	Employee	Contractor	Visitor	General Public	Member	Other
Full Name:						
Address:						
Tel:			*Email:*			

DESCRIPTION OF ACCIDENT / INCIDENT

ACTION TAKEN / ACTIONS WHICH MAY PREVENT FUTURE REOCCURRENCE

WITNESS/ES

Full Name:		*Contact:*	
Full Name:		*Contact:*	
Full Name:		*Contact:*	
Form Completed by:		*Signed:*	
Approved by:		*Signed:*	

ACCIDENT / INCIDENT REPORT FORM

Incident Date:		*Reported by:*		*Report Date:*	
Incident Time:		*Location:*			

Person Involved /Injured:	Employee	Contractor	Visitor	General Public	Member	Other
Full Name:						
Address:						
Tel:			*Email:*			

DESCRIPTION OF ACCIDENT / INCIDENT

ACTION TAKEN / ACTIONS WHICH MAY PREVENT FUTURE REOCCURRENCE

WITNESS/ES

Full Name:		*Contact:*	
Full Name:		*Contact:*	
Full Name:		*Contact:*	
Form Completed by:		*Signed:*	
Approved by:		*Signed:*	

ACCIDENT / INCIDENT REPORT FORM

Incident Date:		*Reported by:*		*Report Date:*	
Incident Time:		*Location:*			

Person Involved /Injured:	Employee	Contractor	Visitor	General Public	Member	Other
Full Name:						
Address:						
Tel:			*Email:*			

DESCRIPTION OF ACCIDENT / INCIDENT

ACTION TAKEN / ACTIONS WHICH MAY PREVENT FUTURE REOCCURRENCE

WITNESS/ES

Full Name:		*Contact:*	
Full Name:		*Contact:*	
Full Name:		*Contact:*	
Form Completed by:		*Signed:*	
Approved by:		*Signed:*	

ACCIDENT / INCIDENT REPORT FORM

Incident Date:		*Reported by:*		*Report Date:*	
Incident Time:		*Location:*			

Person Involved /Injured:	Employee	Contractor	Visitor	General Public	Member	Other
Full Name:						
Address:						
Tel:			*Email:*			

DESCRIPTION OF ACCIDENT / INCIDENT

ACTION TAKEN / ACTIONS WHICH MAY PREVENT FUTURE REOCCURRENCE

WITNESS/ES

Full Name:		*Contact:*	
Full Name:		*Contact:*	
Full Name:		*Contact:*	
Form Completed by:		*Signed:*	
Approved by:		*Signed:*	

ACCIDENT / INCIDENT REPORT FORM

Incident Date:		Reported by:		Report Date:	
Incident Time:		Location:			

Person Involved /Injured:	Employee	Contractor	Visitor	General Public	Member	Other
Full Name:						
Address:						
Tel:			Email:			

DESCRIPTION OF ACCIDENT / INCIDENT

ACTION TAKEN / ACTIONS WHICH MAY PREVENT FUTURE REOCCURRENCE

WITNESS/ES

Full Name:		Contact:	
Full Name:		Contact:	
Full Name:		Contact:	
Form Completed by:		Signed:	
Approved by:		Signed:	

ACCIDENT / INCIDENT REPORT FORM

Incident Date:		*Reported by:*		*Report Date:*	
Incident Time:		*Location:*			

Person Involved /Injured:	Employee	Contractor	Visitor	General Public	Member	Other
Full Name:						
Address:						
Tel:			*Email:*			

DESCRIPTION OF ACCIDENT / INCIDENT

ACTION TAKEN / ACTIONS WHICH MAY PREVENT FUTURE REOCCURRENCE

WITNESS/ES

Full Name:		*Contact:*	
Full Name:		*Contact:*	
Full Name:		*Contact:*	
Form Completed by:		*Signed:*	
Approved by:		*Signed:*	

ACCIDENT / INCIDENT REPORT FORM

Incident Date:		*Reported by:*		*Report Date:*	
Incident Time:		*Location:*			

Person Involved /Injured:	Employee	Contractor	Visitor	General Public	Member	Other
Full Name:						
Address:						
Tel:			*Email:*			

DESCRIPTION OF ACCIDENT / INCIDENT

ACTION TAKEN / ACTIONS WHICH MAY PREVENT FUTURE REOCCURRENCE

WITNESS/ES

Full Name:		*Contact:*	
Full Name:		*Contact:*	
Full Name:		*Contact:*	
Form Completed by:		*Signed:*	
Approved by:		*Signed:*	

ACCIDENT / INCIDENT REPORT FORM

Incident Date:		*Reported by:*		*Report Date:*	
Incident Time:		*Location:*			

Person Involved /Injured:	Employee	Contractor	Visitor	General Public	Member	Other
Full Name:						
Address:						
Tel:			*Email:*			

DESCRIPTION OF ACCIDENT / INCIDENT

ACTION TAKEN / ACTIONS WHICH MAY PREVENT FUTURE REOCCURRENCE

WITNESS/ES

Full Name:		*Contact:*	
Full Name:		*Contact:*	
Full Name:		*Contact:*	
Form Completed by:		*Signed:*	
Approved by:		*Signed:*	

ACCIDENT / INCIDENT REPORT FORM

Incident Date:		*Reported by:*		*Report Date:*	
Incident Time:		*Location:*			

Person Involved /Injured:	Employee	Contractor	Visitor	General Public	Member	Other
Full Name:						
Address:						
Tel:			*Email:*			

DESCRIPTION OF ACCIDENT / INCIDENT

ACTION TAKEN / ACTIONS WHICH MAY PREVENT FUTURE REOCCURRENCE

WITNESS/ES

Full Name:		*Contact:*	
Full Name:		*Contact:*	
Full Name:		*Contact:*	
Form Completed by:		*Signed:*	
Approved by:		*Signed:*	

ACCIDENT / INCIDENT REPORT FORM

Incident Date:		*Reported by:*		*Report Date:*	
Incident Time:		*Location:*			

Person Involved /Injured:	Employee	Contractor	Visitor	General Public	Member	Other
Full Name:						
Address:						
Tel:			*Email:*			

DESCRIPTION OF ACCIDENT / INCIDENT

ACTION TAKEN / ACTIONS WHICH MAY PREVENT FUTURE REOCCURRENCE

WITNESS/ES

Full Name:		*Contact:*	
Full Name:		*Contact:*	
Full Name:		*Contact:*	
Form Completed by:		*Signed:*	
Approved by:		*Signed:*	

ACCIDENT / INCIDENT REPORT FORM

Incident Date:		*Reported by:*		*Report Date:*	
Incident Time:		*Location:*			

Person Involved /Injured:	Employee	Contractor	Visitor	General Public	Member	Other
Full Name:						
Address:						
Tel:			*Email:*			

DESCRIPTION OF ACCIDENT / INCIDENT

ACTION TAKEN / ACTIONS WHICH MAY PREVENT FUTURE REOCCURRENCE

WITNESS/ES

Full Name:		*Contact:*	
Full Name:		*Contact:*	
Full Name:		*Contact:*	
Form Completed by:		*Signed:*	
Approved by:		*Signed:*	

ACCIDENT / INCIDENT REPORT FORM

Incident Date:		*Reported by:*		*Report Date:*	
Incident Time:		*Location:*			

Person Involved /Injured:	Employee	Contractor	Visitor	General Public	Member	Other
Full Name:						
Address:						
Tel:			*Email:*			

DESCRIPTION OF ACCIDENT / INCIDENT

ACTION TAKEN / ACTIONS WHICH MAY PREVENT FUTURE REOCCURRENCE

WITNESS/ES

Full Name:		*Contact:*	
Full Name:		*Contact:*	
Full Name:		*Contact:*	
Form Completed by:		*Signed:*	
Approved by:		*Signed:*	

ACCIDENT / INCIDENT REPORT FORM

Incident Date:		*Reported by:*		*Report Date:*	
Incident Time:		*Location:*			

Person Involved /Injured:	Employee	Contractor	Visitor	General Public	Member	Other
Full Name:						
Address:						
Tel:			*Email:*			

DESCRIPTION OF ACCIDENT / INCIDENT

ACTION TAKEN / ACTIONS WHICH MAY PREVENT FUTURE REOCCURRENCE

WITNESS/ES

Full Name:		*Contact:*	
Full Name:		*Contact:*	
Full Name:		*Contact:*	
Form Completed by:		*Signed:*	
Approved by:		*Signed:*	

ACCIDENT / INCIDENT REPORT FORM

Incident Date:		*Reported by:*		*Report Date:*	
Incident Time:		*Location:*			

Person Involved /Injured:	Employee	Contractor	Visitor	General Public	Member	Other
Full Name:						
Address:						
Tel:			*Email:*			

DESCRIPTION OF ACCIDENT / INCIDENT

ACTION TAKEN / ACTIONS WHICH MAY PREVENT FUTURE REOCCURRENCE

WITNESS/ES

Full Name:		*Contact:*	
Full Name:		*Contact:*	
Full Name:		*Contact:*	
Form Completed by:		*Signed:*	
Approved by:		*Signed:*	

ACCIDENT / INCIDENT REPORT FORM

Incident Date:		*Reported by:*		*Report Date:*	
Incident Time:		*Location:*			

Person Involved /Injured:	Employee	Contractor	Visitor	General Public	Member	Other
Full Name:						
Address:						
Tel:			*Email:*			

DESCRIPTION OF ACCIDENT / INCIDENT

ACTION TAKEN / ACTIONS WHICH MAY PREVENT FUTURE REOCCURRENCE

WITNESS/ES

Full Name:		*Contact:*	
Full Name:		*Contact:*	
Full Name:		*Contact:*	
Form Completed by:		*Signed:*	
Approved by:		*Signed:*	

ACCIDENT / INCIDENT REPORT FORM

Incident Date:		*Reported by:*		*Report Date:*	
Incident Time:		*Location:*			

Person Involved /Injured:	Employee	Contractor	Visitor	General Public	Member	Other
Full Name:						
Address:						
Tel:			*Email:*			

DESCRIPTION OF ACCIDENT / INCIDENT

ACTION TAKEN / ACTIONS WHICH MAY PREVENT FUTURE REOCCURRENCE

WITNESS/ES

Full Name:		*Contact:*	
Full Name:		*Contact:*	
Full Name:		*Contact:*	
Form Completed by:		*Signed:*	
Approved by:		*Signed:*	

ACCIDENT / INCIDENT REPORT FORM

Incident Date:		*Reported by:*			*Report Date:*	
Incident Time:		*Location:*				
Person Involved /Injured:	Employee	Contractor	Visitor	General Public	Member	Other
Full Name:						
Address:						
Tel:			*Email:*			

DESCRIPTION OF ACCIDENT / INCIDENT

ACTION TAKEN / ACTIONS WHICH MAY PREVENT FUTURE REOCCURRENCE

WITNESS/ES

Full Name:		*Contact:*	
Full Name:		*Contact:*	
Full Name:		*Contact:*	
Form Completed by:		*Signed:*	
Approved by:		*Signed:*	

ACCIDENT / INCIDENT REPORT FORM

Incident Date:		*Reported by:*		*Report Date:*	
Incident Time:		*Location:*			

Person Involved /Injured:	Employee	Contractor	Visitor	General Public	Member	Other
Full Name:						
Address:						
Tel:			*Email:*			

DESCRIPTION OF ACCIDENT / INCIDENT

ACTION TAKEN / ACTIONS WHICH MAY PREVENT FUTURE REOCCURRENCE

WITNESS/ES

Full Name:		*Contact:*	
Full Name:		*Contact:*	
Full Name:		*Contact:*	
Form Completed by:		*Signed:*	
Approved by:		*Signed:*	

ACCIDENT / INCIDENT REPORT FORM

Incident Date:		Reported by:		Report Date:	
Incident Time:		Location:			

Person Involved /Injured:	Employee	Contractor	Visitor	General Public	Member	Other
Full Name:						
Address:						
Tel:			Email:			

DESCRIPTION OF ACCIDENT / INCIDENT

ACTION TAKEN / ACTIONS WHICH MAY PREVENT FUTURE REOCCURRENCE

WITNESS/ES

Full Name:		Contact:	
Full Name:		Contact:	
Full Name:		Contact:	
Form Completed by:		Signed:	
Approved by:		Signed:	

ACCIDENT / INCIDENT REPORT FORM

Incident Date:		*Reported by:*			*Report Date:*	
Incident Time:		*Location:*				
Person Involved /Injured:	Employee	Contractor	Visitor	General Public	Member	Other
Full Name:						
Address:						
Tel:			*Email:*			

DESCRIPTION OF ACCIDENT / INCIDENT

ACTION TAKEN / ACTIONS WHICH MAY PREVENT FUTURE REOCCURRENCE

WITNESS/ES

Full Name:		*Contact:*	
Full Name:		*Contact:*	
Full Name:		*Contact:*	
Form Completed by:		*Signed:*	
Approved by:		*Signed:*	

ACCIDENT / INCIDENT REPORT FORM

Incident Date:		*Reported by:*		*Report Date:*	
Incident Time:		*Location:*			

Person Involved /Injured:	Employee	Contractor	Visitor	General Public	Member	Other
Full Name:						
Address:						
Tel:			*Email:*			

DESCRIPTION OF ACCIDENT / INCIDENT

ACTION TAKEN / ACTIONS WHICH MAY PREVENT FUTURE REOCCURRENCE

WITNESS/ES

Full Name:		*Contact:*	
Full Name:		*Contact:*	
Full Name:		*Contact:*	
Form Completed by:		*Signed:*	
Approved by:		*Signed:*	

ACCIDENT / INCIDENT REPORT FORM

Incident Date:		*Reported by:*		*Report Date:*	
Incident Time:		*Location:*			

Person Involved /Injured:	Employee	Contractor	Visitor	General Public	Member	Other
Full Name:						
Address:						
Tel:			*Email:*			

DESCRIPTION OF ACCIDENT / INCIDENT

ACTION TAKEN / ACTIONS WHICH MAY PREVENT FUTURE REOCCURRENCE

WITNESS/ES

Full Name:		*Contact:*	
Full Name:		*Contact:*	
Full Name:		*Contact:*	
Form Completed by:		*Signed:*	
Approved by:		*Signed:*	

ACCIDENT / INCIDENT REPORT FORM

Incident Date:		*Reported by:*		*Report Date:*	
Incident Time:		*Location:*			

Person Involved /Injured:	Employee	Contractor	Visitor	General Public	Member	Other
Full Name:						
Address:						
Tel:			*Email:*			

DESCRIPTION OF ACCIDENT / INCIDENT

ACTION TAKEN / ACTIONS WHICH MAY PREVENT FUTURE REOCCURRENCE

WITNESS/ES

Full Name:		*Contact:*	
Full Name:		*Contact:*	
Full Name:		*Contact:*	
Form Completed by:		*Signed:*	
Approved by:		*Signed:*	

ACCIDENT / INCIDENT REPORT FORM

Incident Date:		*Reported by:*		*Report Date:*	
Incident Time:		*Location:*			

Person Involved /Injured:	Employee	Contractor	Visitor	General Public	Member	Other
Full Name:						
Address:						
Tel:			*Email:*			

DESCRIPTION OF ACCIDENT / INCIDENT

ACTION TAKEN / ACTIONS WHICH MAY PREVENT FUTURE REOCCURRENCE

WITNESS/ES

Full Name:		*Contact:*	
Full Name:		*Contact:*	
Full Name:		*Contact:*	
Form Completed by:		*Signed:*	
Approved by:		*Signed:*	

ACCIDENT / INCIDENT REPORT FORM

Incident Date:		*Reported by:*		*Report Date:*	
Incident Time:		*Location:*			

Person Involved /Injured:	Employee	Contractor	Visitor	General Public	Member	Other
Full Name:						
Address:						
Tel:			*Email:*			

DESCRIPTION OF ACCIDENT / INCIDENT

ACTION TAKEN / ACTIONS WHICH MAY PREVENT FUTURE REOCCURRENCE

WITNESS/ES

Full Name:		*Contact:*	
Full Name:		*Contact:*	
Full Name:		*Contact:*	
Form Completed by:		*Signed:*	
Approved by:		*Signed:*	

ACCIDENT / INCIDENT REPORT FORM

Incident Date:		*Reported by:*		*Report Date:*	
Incident Time:		*Location:*			

Person Involved /Injured:	Employee	Contractor	Visitor	General Public	Member	Other
Full Name:						
Address:						
Tel:			*Email:*			

DESCRIPTION OF ACCIDENT / INCIDENT

ACTION TAKEN / ACTIONS WHICH MAY PREVENT FUTURE REOCCURRENCE

WITNESS/ES

Full Name:		*Contact:*	
Full Name:		*Contact:*	
Full Name:		*Contact:*	
Form Completed by:		*Signed:*	
Approved by:		*Signed:*	

ACCIDENT / INCIDENT REPORT FORM

Incident Date:		*Reported by:*		*Report Date:*	
Incident Time:		*Location:*			

Person Involved /Injured:	Employee	Contractor	Visitor	General Public	Member	Other
Full Name:						
Address:						
Tel:			*Email:*			

DESCRIPTION OF ACCIDENT / INCIDENT

ACTION TAKEN / ACTIONS WHICH MAY PREVENT FUTURE REOCCURRENCE

WITNESS/ES

Full Name:		*Contact:*	
Full Name:		*Contact:*	
Full Name:		*Contact:*	
Form Completed by:		*Signed:*	
Approved by:		*Signed:*	

ACCIDENT / INCIDENT REPORT FORM

Incident Date:		*Reported by:*		*Report Date:*	
Incident Time:		*Location:*			

Person Involved /Injured:	Employee	Contractor	Visitor	General Public	Member	Other
Full Name:						
Address:						
Tel:			*Email:*			

DESCRIPTION OF ACCIDENT / INCIDENT

ACTION TAKEN / ACTIONS WHICH MAY PREVENT FUTURE REOCCURRENCE

WITNESS/ES

Full Name:		*Contact:*	
Full Name:		*Contact:*	
Full Name:		*Contact:*	
Form Completed by:		*Signed:*	
Approved by:		*Signed:*	

ACCIDENT / INCIDENT REPORT FORM

Incident Date:		*Reported by:*		*Report Date:*	
Incident Time:		*Location:*			

Person Involved /Injured:	Employee	Contractor	Visitor	General Public	Member	Other
Full Name:						
Address:						
Tel:		*Email:*				

DESCRIPTION OF ACCIDENT / INCIDENT

ACTION TAKEN / ACTIONS WHICH MAY PREVENT FUTURE REOCCURRENCE

WITNESS/ES

Full Name:		*Contact:*	
Full Name:		*Contact:*	
Full Name:		*Contact:*	
Form Completed by:		*Signed:*	
Approved by:		*Signed:*	

ACCIDENT / INCIDENT REPORT FORM

Incident Date:		*Reported by:*		*Report Date:*	
Incident Time:		*Location:*			

Person Involved /Injured:	Employee	Contractor	Visitor	General Public	Member	Other
Full Name:						
Address:						
Tel:			*Email:*			

DESCRIPTION OF ACCIDENT / INCIDENT

ACTION TAKEN / ACTIONS WHICH MAY PREVENT FUTURE REOCCURRENCE

WITNESS/ES

Full Name:		*Contact:*	
Full Name:		*Contact:*	
Full Name:		*Contact:*	
Form Completed by:		*Signed:*	
Approved by:		*Signed:*	

ACCIDENT / INCIDENT REPORT FORM

Incident Date:		*Reported by:*		*Report Date:*	
Incident Time:		*Location:*			

Person Involved /Injured:	Employee	Contractor	Visitor	General Public	Member	Other
Full Name:						
Address:						
Tel:			*Email:*			

DESCRIPTION OF ACCIDENT / INCIDENT

ACTION TAKEN / ACTIONS WHICH MAY PREVENT FUTURE REOCCURRENCE

WITNESS/ES

Full Name:		*Contact:*	
Full Name:		*Contact:*	
Full Name:		*Contact:*	
Form Completed by:		*Signed:*	
Approved by:		*Signed:*	

ACCIDENT / INCIDENT REPORT FORM

Incident Date:		*Reported by:*		*Report Date:*	
Incident Time:		*Location:*			

Person Involved /Injured:	Employee	Contractor	Visitor	General Public	Member	Other
Full Name:						
Address:						
Tel:			*Email:*			

DESCRIPTION OF ACCIDENT / INCIDENT

ACTION TAKEN / ACTIONS WHICH MAY PREVENT FUTURE REOCCURRENCE

WITNESS/ES

Full Name:		*Contact:*	
Full Name:		*Contact:*	
Full Name:		*Contact:*	
Form Completed by:		*Signed:*	
Approved by:		*Signed:*	

ACCIDENT / INCIDENT REPORT FORM

Incident Date:		*Reported by:*		*Report Date:*	
Incident Time:		*Location:*			

Person Involved /Injured:	Employee	Contractor	Visitor	General Public	Member	Other
Full Name:						
Address:						
Tel:			*Email:*			

DESCRIPTION OF ACCIDENT / INCIDENT

ACTION TAKEN / ACTIONS WHICH MAY PREVENT FUTURE REOCCURRENCE

WITNESS/ES

Full Name:		*Contact:*	
Full Name:		*Contact:*	
Full Name:		*Contact:*	
Form Completed by:		*Signed:*	
Approved by:		*Signed:*	

ACCIDENT / INCIDENT REPORT FORM

Incident Date:		*Reported by:*		*Report Date:*	
Incident Time:		*Location:*			

Person Involved /Injured:	Employee	Contractor	Visitor	General Public	Member	Other
Full Name:						
Address:						
Tel:			*Email:*			

DESCRIPTION OF ACCIDENT / INCIDENT

ACTION TAKEN / ACTIONS WHICH MAY PREVENT FUTURE REOCCURRENCE

WITNESS/ES

Full Name:		*Contact:*	
Full Name:		*Contact:*	
Full Name:		*Contact:*	
Form Completed by:		*Signed:*	
Approved by:		*Signed:*	

ACCIDENT / INCIDENT REPORT FORM

Incident Date:		*Reported by:*		*Report Date:*	
Incident Time:		*Location:*			

Person Involved /Injured:	Employee	Contractor	Visitor	General Public	Member	Other
Full Name:						
Address:						
Tel:			*Email:*			

DESCRIPTION OF ACCIDENT / INCIDENT

ACTION TAKEN / ACTIONS WHICH MAY PREVENT FUTURE REOCCURRENCE

WITNESS/ES

Full Name:		*Contact:*	
Full Name:		*Contact:*	
Full Name:		*Contact:*	
Form Completed by:		*Signed:*	
Approved by:		*Signed:*	

ACCIDENT / INCIDENT REPORT FORM

Incident Date:		*Reported by:*		*Report Date:*	
Incident Time:		*Location:*			

Person Involved /Injured:	Employee	Contractor	Visitor	General Public	Member	Other
Full Name:						
Address:						
Tel:			*Email:*			

DESCRIPTION OF ACCIDENT / INCIDENT

ACTION TAKEN / ACTIONS WHICH MAY PREVENT FUTURE REOCCURRENCE

WITNESS/ES

Full Name:		*Contact:*	
Full Name:		*Contact:*	
Full Name:		*Contact:*	
Form Completed by:		*Signed:*	
Approved by:		*Signed:*	

ACCIDENT / INCIDENT REPORT FORM

Incident Date:		*Reported by:*		*Report Date:*	
Incident Time:		*Location:*			

Person Involved /Injured:	Employee	Contractor	Visitor	General Public	Member	Other
Full Name:						
Address:						
Tel:			*Email:*			

DESCRIPTION OF ACCIDENT / INCIDENT

ACTION TAKEN / ACTIONS WHICH MAY PREVENT FUTURE REOCCURRENCE

WITNESS/ES

Full Name:		*Contact:*	
Full Name:		*Contact:*	
Full Name:		*Contact:*	
Form Completed by:		*Signed:*	
Approved by:		*Signed:*	

ACCIDENT / INCIDENT REPORT FORM

Incident Date:		*Reported by:*			*Report Date:*	
Incident Time:		*Location:*				
Person Involved /Injured:	Employee	Contractor	Visitor	General Public	Member	Other
Full Name:						
Address:						
Tel:			*Email:*			

DESCRIPTION OF ACCIDENT / INCIDENT

ACTION TAKEN / ACTIONS WHICH MAY PREVENT FUTURE REOCCURRENCE

WITNESS/ES

Full Name:		*Contact:*	
Full Name:		*Contact:*	
Full Name:		*Contact:*	
Form Completed by:		*Signed:*	
Approved by:		*Signed:*	

ACCIDENT / INCIDENT REPORT FORM

Incident Date:		*Reported by:*		*Report Date:*	
Incident Time:		*Location:*			

Person Involved /Injured:	Employee	Contractor	Visitor	General Public	Member	Other
Full Name:						
Address:						
Tel:			*Email:*			

DESCRIPTION OF ACCIDENT / INCIDENT

ACTION TAKEN / ACTIONS WHICH MAY PREVENT FUTURE REOCCURRENCE

WITNESS/ES

Full Name:		*Contact:*	
Full Name:		*Contact:*	
Full Name:		*Contact:*	
Form Completed by:		*Signed:*	
Approved by:		*Signed:*	

ACCIDENT / INCIDENT REPORT FORM

Incident Date:		*Reported by:*		*Report Date:*	
Incident Time:		*Location:*			

Person Involved /Injured:	Employee	Contractor	Visitor	General Public	Member	Other
Full Name:						
Address:						
Tel:			*Email:*			

DESCRIPTION OF ACCIDENT / INCIDENT

ACTION TAKEN / ACTIONS WHICH MAY PREVENT FUTURE REOCCURRENCE

WITNESS/ES

Full Name:		*Contact:*	
Full Name:		*Contact:*	
Full Name:		*Contact:*	
Form Completed by:		*Signed:*	
Approved by:		*Signed:*	

ACCIDENT / INCIDENT REPORT FORM

Incident Date:		*Reported by:*		*Report Date:*	
Incident Time:		*Location:*			

Person Involved /Injured:	Employee	Contractor	Visitor	General Public	Member	Other
Full Name:						
Address:						
Tel:			*Email:*			

DESCRIPTION OF ACCIDENT / INCIDENT

ACTION TAKEN / ACTIONS WHICH MAY PREVENT FUTURE REOCCURRENCE

WITNESS/ES

Full Name:		*Contact:*	
Full Name:		*Contact:*	
Full Name:		*Contact:*	
Form Completed by:		*Signed:*	
Approved by:		*Signed:*	

ACCIDENT / INCIDENT REPORT FORM

Incident Date:		*Reported by:*		*Report Date:*	
Incident Time:		*Location:*			

Person Involved /Injured:	Employee	Contractor	Visitor	General Public	Member	Other
Full Name:						
Address:						
Tel:			*Email:*			

DESCRIPTION OF ACCIDENT / INCIDENT

ACTION TAKEN / ACTIONS WHICH MAY PREVENT FUTURE REOCCURRENCE

WITNESS/ES

Full Name:		*Contact:*	
Full Name:		*Contact:*	
Full Name:		*Contact:*	
Form Completed by:		*Signed:*	
Approved by:		*Signed:*	

ACCIDENT / INCIDENT REPORT FORM

Incident Date:		*Reported by:*		*Report Date:*	
Incident Time:		*Location:*			

Person Involved /Injured:	Employee	Contractor	Visitor	General Public	Member	Other
Full Name:						
Address:						
Tel:			*Email:*			

DESCRIPTION OF ACCIDENT / INCIDENT

ACTION TAKEN / ACTIONS WHICH MAY PREVENT FUTURE REOCCURRENCE

WITNESS/ES

Full Name:		*Contact:*	
Full Name:		*Contact:*	
Full Name:		*Contact:*	
Form Completed by:		*Signed:*	
Approved by:		*Signed:*	

ACCIDENT / INCIDENT REPORT FORM

Incident Date:		*Reported by:*		*Report Date:*	
Incident Time:		*Location:*			

Person Involved /Injured:	Employee	Contractor	Visitor	General Public	Member	Other
Full Name:						
Address:						
Tel:			*Email:*			

DESCRIPTION OF ACCIDENT / INCIDENT

ACTION TAKEN / ACTIONS WHICH MAY PREVENT FUTURE REOCCURRENCE

WITNESS/ES

Full Name:		*Contact:*	
Full Name:		*Contact:*	
Full Name:		*Contact:*	
Form Completed by:		*Signed:*	
Approved by:		*Signed:*	

ACCIDENT / INCIDENT REPORT FORM

Incident Date:		*Reported by:*		*Report Date:*	
Incident Time:		*Location:*			

Person Involved /Injured:	Employee	Contractor	Visitor	General Public	Member	Other
Full Name:						
Address:						
Tel:			*Email:*			

DESCRIPTION OF ACCIDENT / INCIDENT

ACTION TAKEN / ACTIONS WHICH MAY PREVENT FUTURE REOCCURRENCE

WITNESS/ES

Full Name:		*Contact:*	
Full Name:		*Contact:*	
Full Name:		*Contact:*	
Form Completed by:		*Signed:*	
Approved by:		*Signed:*	

ACCIDENT / INCIDENT REPORT FORM

Incident Date:		*Reported by:*		*Report Date:*	
Incident Time:		*Location:*			

Person Involved /Injured:	Employee	Contractor	Visitor	General Public	Member	Other
Full Name:						
Address:						
Tel:			*Email:*			

DESCRIPTION OF ACCIDENT / INCIDENT

ACTION TAKEN / ACTIONS WHICH MAY PREVENT FUTURE REOCCURRENCE

WITNESS/ES

Full Name:		*Contact:*	
Full Name:		*Contact:*	
Full Name:		*Contact:*	
Form Completed by:		*Signed:*	
Approved by:		*Signed:*	

ACCIDENT / INCIDENT REPORT FORM

Incident Date:		*Reported by:*		*Report Date:*	
Incident Time:		*Location:*			

Person Involved /Injured:	Employee	Contractor	Visitor	General Public	Member	Other
Full Name:						
Address:						
Tel:			*Email:*			

DESCRIPTION OF ACCIDENT / INCIDENT

ACTION TAKEN / ACTIONS WHICH MAY PREVENT FUTURE REOCCURRENCE

WITNESS/ES

Full Name:		*Contact:*	
Full Name:		*Contact:*	
Full Name:		*Contact:*	
Form Completed by:		*Signed:*	
Approved by:		*Signed:*	

ACCIDENT / INCIDENT REPORT FORM

Incident Date:		*Reported by:*		*Report Date:*	
Incident Time:		*Location:*			

Person Involved /Injured:	Employee	Contractor	Visitor	General Public	Member	Other
Full Name:						
Address:						
Tel:			*Email:*			

DESCRIPTION OF ACCIDENT / INCIDENT

ACTION TAKEN / ACTIONS WHICH MAY PREVENT FUTURE REOCCURRENCE

WITNESS/ES

Full Name:		*Contact:*	
Full Name:		*Contact:*	
Full Name:		*Contact:*	
Form Completed by:		*Signed:*	
Approved by:		*Signed:*	

ACCIDENT / INCIDENT REPORT FORM

Incident Date:		*Reported by:*		*Report Date:*	
Incident Time:		*Location:*			

Person Involved /Injured:	Employee	Contractor	Visitor	General Public	Member	Other
Full Name:						
Address:						
Tel:			*Email:*			

DESCRIPTION OF ACCIDENT / INCIDENT

ACTION TAKEN / ACTIONS WHICH MAY PREVENT FUTURE REOCCURRENCE

WITNESS/ES

Full Name:		*Contact:*	
Full Name:		*Contact:*	
Full Name:		*Contact:*	
Form Completed by:		*Signed:*	
Approved by:		*Signed:*	

ACCIDENT / INCIDENT REPORT FORM

Incident Date:		*Reported by:*			*Report Date:*	
Incident Time:		*Location:*				
Person Involved /Injured:	Employee	Contractor	Visitor	General Public	Member	Other
Full Name:						
Address:						
Tel:			*Email:*			

DESCRIPTION OF ACCIDENT / INCIDENT

ACTION TAKEN / ACTIONS WHICH MAY PREVENT FUTURE REOCCURRENCE

WITNESS/ES

Full Name:		*Contact:*	
Full Name:		*Contact:*	
Full Name:		*Contact:*	
Form Completed by:		*Signed:*	
Approved by:		*Signed:*	

ACCIDENT / INCIDENT REPORT FORM

Incident Date:		*Reported by:*		*Report Date:*	
Incident Time:		*Location:*			

Person Involved /Injured:	Employee	Contractor	Visitor	General Public	Member	Other
Full Name:						
Address:						
Tel:			*Email:*			

DESCRIPTION OF ACCIDENT / INCIDENT

ACTION TAKEN / ACTIONS WHICH MAY PREVENT FUTURE REOCCURRENCE

WITNESS/ES

Full Name:		*Contact:*	
Full Name:		*Contact:*	
Full Name:		*Contact:*	
Form Completed by:		*Signed:*	
Approved by:		*Signed:*	

ACCIDENT / INCIDENT REPORT FORM

Incident Date:		*Reported by:*		*Report Date:*	
Incident Time:		*Location:*			

Person Involved /Injured:	Employee	Contractor	Visitor	General Public	Member	Other
Full Name:						
Address:						
Tel:			*Email:*			

DESCRIPTION OF ACCIDENT / INCIDENT

ACTION TAKEN / ACTIONS WHICH MAY PREVENT FUTURE REOCCURRENCE

WITNESS/ES

Full Name:		*Contact:*	
Full Name:		*Contact:*	
Full Name:		*Contact:*	
Form Completed by:		*Signed:*	
Approved by:		*Signed:*	

ACCIDENT / INCIDENT REPORT FORM

Incident Date:		*Reported by:*			*Report Date:*	
Incident Time:		*Location:*				
Person Involved /Injured:	Employee	Contractor	Visitor	General Public	Member	Other
Full Name:						
Address:						
Tel:			*Email:*			

DESCRIPTION OF ACCIDENT / INCIDENT

ACTION TAKEN / ACTIONS WHICH MAY PREVENT FUTURE REOCCURRENCE

WITNESS/ES

Full Name:		*Contact:*	
Full Name:		*Contact:*	
Full Name:		*Contact:*	
Form Completed by:		*Signed:*	
Approved by:		*Signed:*	

ACCIDENT / INCIDENT REPORT FORM

Incident Date:		*Reported by:*		*Report Date:*	
Incident Time:		*Location:*			

Person Involved /Injured:	Employee	Contractor	Visitor	General Public	Member	Other
Full Name:						
Address:						
Tel:			*Email:*			

DESCRIPTION OF ACCIDENT / INCIDENT

ACTION TAKEN / ACTIONS WHICH MAY PREVENT FUTURE REOCCURRENCE

WITNESS/ES

Full Name:		*Contact:*	
Full Name:		*Contact:*	
Full Name:		*Contact:*	
Form Completed by:		*Signed:*	
Approved by:		*Signed:*	

ACCIDENT / INCIDENT REPORT FORM

Incident Date:		*Reported by:*		*Report Date:*	
Incident Time:		*Location:*			

Person Involved /Injured:	Employee	Contractor	Visitor	General Public	Member	Other
Full Name:						
Address:						
Tel:			*Email:*			

DESCRIPTION OF ACCIDENT / INCIDENT

ACTION TAKEN / ACTIONS WHICH MAY PREVENT FUTURE REOCCURRENCE

WITNESS/ES

Full Name:		*Contact:*	
Full Name:		*Contact:*	
Full Name:		*Contact:*	
Form Completed by:		*Signed:*	
Approved by:		*Signed:*	

ACCIDENT / INCIDENT REPORT FORM

Incident Date:		*Reported by:*		*Report Date:*	
Incident Time:		*Location:*			

Person Involved /Injured:	Employee	Contractor	Visitor	General Public	Member	Other
Full Name:						
Address:						
Tel:			*Email:*			

DESCRIPTION OF ACCIDENT / INCIDENT

ACTION TAKEN / ACTIONS WHICH MAY PREVENT FUTURE REOCCURRENCE

WITNESS/ES

Full Name:		*Contact:*	
Full Name:		*Contact:*	
Full Name:		*Contact:*	
Form Completed by:		*Signed:*	
Approved by:		*Signed:*	

ACCIDENT / INCIDENT REPORT FORM

Incident Date:		*Reported by:*		*Report Date:*	
Incident Time:		*Location:*			

Person Involved /Injured:	Employee	Contractor	Visitor	General Public	Member	Other
Full Name:						
Address:						
Tel:			*Email:*			

DESCRIPTION OF ACCIDENT / INCIDENT

ACTION TAKEN / ACTIONS WHICH MAY PREVENT FUTURE REOCCURRENCE

WITNESS/ES

Full Name:		*Contact:*	
Full Name:		*Contact:*	
Full Name:		*Contact:*	
Form Completed by:		*Signed:*	
Approved by:		*Signed:*	

ACCIDENT / INCIDENT REPORT FORM

Incident Date:		*Reported by:*		*Report Date:*	
Incident Time:		*Location:*			

Person Involved /Injured:	Employee	Contractor	Visitor	General Public	Member	Other
Full Name:						
Address:						
Tel:			*Email:*			

DESCRIPTION OF ACCIDENT / INCIDENT

ACTION TAKEN / ACTIONS WHICH MAY PREVENT FUTURE REOCCURRENCE

WITNESS/ES

Full Name:		*Contact:*	
Full Name:		*Contact:*	
Full Name:		*Contact:*	
Form Completed by:		*Signed:*	
Approved by:		*Signed:*	

ACCIDENT / INCIDENT REPORT FORM

Incident Date:		*Reported by:*		*Report Date:*	
Incident Time:		*Location:*			

Person Involved /Injured:	Employee	Contractor	Visitor	General Public	Member	Other
Full Name:						
Address:						
Tel:			*Email:*			

DESCRIPTION OF ACCIDENT / INCIDENT

ACTION TAKEN / ACTIONS WHICH MAY PREVENT FUTURE REOCCURRENCE

WITNESS/ES

Full Name:		*Contact:*	
Full Name:		*Contact:*	
Full Name:		*Contact:*	
Form Completed by:		*Signed:*	
Approved by:		*Signed:*	

ACCIDENT / INCIDENT REPORT FORM

Incident Date:		*Reported by:*		*Report Date:*	
Incident Time:		*Location:*			

Person Involved /Injured:	Employee	Contractor	Visitor	General Public	Member	Other
Full Name:						
Address:						
Tel:			*Email:*			

DESCRIPTION OF ACCIDENT / INCIDENT

ACTION TAKEN / ACTIONS WHICH MAY PREVENT FUTURE REOCCURRENCE

WITNESS/ES

Full Name:		*Contact:*	
Full Name:		*Contact:*	
Full Name:		*Contact:*	
Form Completed by:		*Signed:*	
Approved by:		*Signed:*	

ACCIDENT / INCIDENT REPORT FORM

Incident Date:		*Reported by:*		*Report Date:*	
Incident Time:		*Location:*			

Person Involved /Injured:	Employee	Contractor	Visitor	General Public	Member	Other
Full Name:						
Address:						
Tel:			*Email:*			

DESCRIPTION OF ACCIDENT / INCIDENT

ACTION TAKEN / ACTIONS WHICH MAY PREVENT FUTURE REOCCURRENCE

WITNESS/ES

Full Name:		*Contact:*	
Full Name:		*Contact:*	
Full Name:		*Contact:*	
Form Completed by:		*Signed:*	
Approved by:		*Signed:*	

ACCIDENT / INCIDENT REPORT FORM

Incident Date:		*Reported by:*		*Report Date:*	
Incident Time:		*Location:*			

Person Involved /Injured:	Employee	Contractor	Visitor	General Public	Member	Other
Full Name:						
Address:						
Tel:			*Email:*			

DESCRIPTION OF ACCIDENT / INCIDENT

ACTION TAKEN / ACTIONS WHICH MAY PREVENT FUTURE REOCCURRENCE

WITNESS/ES

Full Name:		*Contact:*	
Full Name:		*Contact:*	
Full Name:		*Contact:*	
Form Completed by:		*Signed:*	
Approved by:		*Signed:*	

ACCIDENT / INCIDENT REPORT FORM

Incident Date:		*Reported by:*		*Report Date:*	
Incident Time:		*Location:*			

Person Involved /Injured:	Employee	Contractor	Visitor	General Public	Member	Other
Full Name:						
Address:						
Tel:			*Email:*			

DESCRIPTION OF ACCIDENT / INCIDENT

ACTION TAKEN / ACTIONS WHICH MAY PREVENT FUTURE REOCCURRENCE

WITNESS/ES

Full Name:		*Contact:*	
Full Name:		*Contact:*	
Full Name:		*Contact:*	
Form Completed by:		*Signed:*	
Approved by:		*Signed:*	

ACCIDENT / INCIDENT REPORT FORM

Incident Date:		*Reported by:*		*Report Date:*	
Incident Time:		*Location:*			
Person Involved /Injured:	Employee	Contractor	Visitor	General Public	Member	Other
Full Name:						
Address:						
Tel:			*Email:*			

DESCRIPTION OF ACCIDENT / INCIDENT

ACTION TAKEN / ACTIONS WHICH MAY PREVENT FUTURE REOCCURRENCE

WITNESS/ES

Full Name:		*Contact:*	
Full Name:		*Contact:*	
Full Name:		*Contact:*	
Form Completed by:		*Signed:*	
Approved by:		*Signed:*	

ACCIDENT / INCIDENT REPORT FORM

Incident Date:		*Reported by:*		*Report Date:*	
Incident Time:		*Location:*			

Person Involved /Injured:	Employee	Contractor	Visitor	General Public	Member	Other
Full Name:						
Address:						
Tel:		*Email:*				

DESCRIPTION OF ACCIDENT / INCIDENT

ACTION TAKEN / ACTIONS WHICH MAY PREVENT FUTURE REOCCURRENCE

WITNESS/ES

Full Name:		*Contact:*	
Full Name:		*Contact:*	
Full Name:		*Contact:*	
Form Completed by:		*Signed:*	
Approved by:		*Signed:*	

ACCIDENT / INCIDENT REPORT FORM

Incident Date:		*Reported by:*		*Report Date:*	
Incident Time:		*Location:*			

Person Involved /Injured:	Employee	Contractor	Visitor	General Public	Member	Other
Full Name:						
Address:						
Tel:			*Email:*			

DESCRIPTION OF ACCIDENT / INCIDENT

ACTION TAKEN / ACTIONS WHICH MAY PREVENT FUTURE REOCCURRENCE

WITNESS/ES

Full Name:		*Contact:*	
Full Name:		*Contact:*	
Full Name:		*Contact:*	
Form Completed by:		*Signed:*	
Approved by:		*Signed:*	

ACCIDENT / INCIDENT REPORT FORM

Incident Date:		*Reported by:*		*Report Date:*	
Incident Time:		*Location:*			

Person Involved /Injured:	Employee	Contractor	Visitor	General Public	Member	Other
Full Name:						
Address:						
Tel:			*Email:*			

DESCRIPTION OF ACCIDENT / INCIDENT

ACTION TAKEN / ACTIONS WHICH MAY PREVENT FUTURE REOCCURRENCE

WITNESS/ES

Full Name:		*Contact:*	
Full Name:		*Contact:*	
Full Name:		*Contact:*	
Form Completed by:		*Signed:*	
Approved by:		*Signed:*	

ACCIDENT / INCIDENT REPORT FORM

Incident Date:		*Reported by:*		*Report Date:*	
Incident Time:		*Location:*			

Person Involved /Injured:	Employee	Contractor	Visitor	General Public	Member	Other
Full Name:						
Address:						
Tel:			*Email:*			

DESCRIPTION OF ACCIDENT / INCIDENT

ACTION TAKEN / ACTIONS WHICH MAY PREVENT FUTURE REOCCURRENCE

WITNESS/ES

Full Name:		*Contact:*	
Full Name:		*Contact:*	
Full Name:		*Contact:*	
Form Completed by:		*Signed:*	
Approved by:		*Signed:*	

ACCIDENT / INCIDENT REPORT FORM

Incident Date:		*Reported by:*		*Report Date:*	
Incident Time:		*Location:*			

Person Involved /Injured:	Employee	Contractor	Visitor	General Public	Member	Other
Full Name:						
Address:						
Tel:			*Email:*			

DESCRIPTION OF ACCIDENT / INCIDENT

ACTION TAKEN / ACTIONS WHICH MAY PREVENT FUTURE REOCCURRENCE

WITNESS/ES

Full Name:		*Contact:*	
Full Name:		*Contact:*	
Full Name:		*Contact:*	
Form Completed by:		*Signed:*	
Approved by:		*Signed:*	

ACCIDENT / INCIDENT REPORT FORM

Incident Date:		*Reported by:*		*Report Date:*	
Incident Time:		*Location:*			

Person Involved /Injured:	Employee	Contractor	Visitor	General Public	Member	Other
Full Name:						
Address:						
Tel:			*Email:*			

DESCRIPTION OF ACCIDENT / INCIDENT

ACTION TAKEN / ACTIONS WHICH MAY PREVENT FUTURE REOCCURRENCE

WITNESS/ES

Full Name:		*Contact:*	
Full Name:		*Contact:*	
Full Name:		*Contact:*	
Form Completed by:		*Signed:*	
Approved by:		*Signed:*	

ACCIDENT / INCIDENT REPORT FORM

Incident Date:		*Reported by:*		*Report Date:*	
Incident Time:		*Location:*			

Person Involved /Injured:	Employee	Contractor	Visitor	General Public	Member	Other
Full Name:						
Address:						
Tel:			*Email:*			

DESCRIPTION OF ACCIDENT / INCIDENT

ACTION TAKEN / ACTIONS WHICH MAY PREVENT FUTURE REOCCURRENCE

WITNESS/ES

Full Name:		*Contact:*	
Full Name:		*Contact:*	
Full Name:		*Contact:*	
Form Completed by:		*Signed:*	
Approved by:		*Signed:*	

ACCIDENT / INCIDENT REPORT FORM

Incident Date:		*Reported by:*		*Report Date:*	
Incident Time:		*Location:*			

Person Involved /Injured:	Employee	Contractor	Visitor	General Public	Member	Other
Full Name:						
Address:						
Tel:			*Email:*			

DESCRIPTION OF ACCIDENT / INCIDENT

ACTION TAKEN / ACTIONS WHICH MAY PREVENT FUTURE REOCCURRENCE

WITNESS/ES

Full Name:		*Contact:*	
Full Name:		*Contact:*	
Full Name:		*Contact:*	
Form Completed by:		*Signed:*	
Approved by:		*Signed:*	

ACCIDENT / INCIDENT REPORT FORM

Incident Date:		*Reported by:*		*Report Date:*	
Incident Time:		*Location:*			

Person Involved /Injured:	Employee	Contractor	Visitor	General Public	Member	Other
Full Name:						
Address:						
Tel:			*Email:*			

DESCRIPTION OF ACCIDENT / INCIDENT

ACTION TAKEN / ACTIONS WHICH MAY PREVENT FUTURE REOCCURRENCE

WITNESS/ES

Full Name:		*Contact:*	
Full Name:		*Contact:*	
Full Name:		*Contact:*	
Form Completed by:		*Signed:*	
Approved by:		*Signed:*	

ACCIDENT / INCIDENT REPORT FORM

Incident Date:		*Reported by:*		*Report Date:*	
Incident Time:		*Location:*			

Person Involved /Injured:	Employee	Contractor	Visitor	General Public	Member	Other
Full Name:						
Address:						
Tel:			*Email:*			

DESCRIPTION OF ACCIDENT / INCIDENT

ACTION TAKEN / ACTIONS WHICH MAY PREVENT FUTURE REOCCURRENCE

WITNESS/ES

Full Name:		*Contact:*	
Full Name:		*Contact:*	
Full Name:		*Contact:*	
Form Completed by:		*Signed:*	
Approved by:		*Signed:*	

ACCIDENT / INCIDENT REPORT FORM

Incident Date:		*Reported by:*		*Report Date:*	
Incident Time:		*Location:*			

Person Involved /Injured:	Employee	Contractor	Visitor	General Public	Member	Other
Full Name:						
Address:						
Tel:			*Email:*			

DESCRIPTION OF ACCIDENT / INCIDENT

ACTION TAKEN / ACTIONS WHICH MAY PREVENT FUTURE REOCCURRENCE

WITNESS/ES

Full Name:		*Contact:*	
Full Name:		*Contact:*	
Full Name:		*Contact:*	
Form Completed by:		*Signed:*	
Approved by:		*Signed:*	

ACCIDENT / INCIDENT REPORT FORM

Incident Date:		*Reported by:*		*Report Date:*	
Incident Time:		*Location:*			

Person Involved /Injured:	Employee	Contractor	Visitor	General Public	Member	Other
Full Name:						
Address:						
Tel:			*Email:*			

DESCRIPTION OF ACCIDENT / INCIDENT

ACTION TAKEN / ACTIONS WHICH MAY PREVENT FUTURE REOCCURRENCE

WITNESS/ES

Full Name:		*Contact:*	
Full Name:		*Contact:*	
Full Name:		*Contact:*	
Form Completed by:		*Signed:*	
Approved by:		*Signed:*	

ACCIDENT / INCIDENT REPORT FORM

Incident Date:		*Reported by:*		*Report Date:*	
Incident Time:		*Location:*			

Person Involved /Injured:	Employee	Contractor	Visitor	General Public	Member	Other
Full Name:						
Address:						
Tel:			*Email:*			

DESCRIPTION OF ACCIDENT / INCIDENT

ACTION TAKEN / ACTIONS WHICH MAY PREVENT FUTURE REOCCURRENCE

WITNESS/ES

Full Name:		*Contact:*	
Full Name:		*Contact:*	
Full Name:		*Contact:*	
Form Completed by:		*Signed:*	
Approved by:		*Signed:*	

ACCIDENT / INCIDENT REPORT FORM

Incident Date:		*Reported by:*		*Report Date:*	
Incident Time:		*Location:*			

Person Involved /Injured:	Employee	Contractor	Visitor	General Public	Member	Other
Full Name:						
Address:						
Tel:			*Email:*			

DESCRIPTION OF ACCIDENT / INCIDENT

ACTION TAKEN / ACTIONS WHICH MAY PREVENT FUTURE REOCCURRENCE

WITNESS/ES

Full Name:		*Contact:*	
Full Name:		*Contact:*	
Full Name:		*Contact:*	
Form Completed by:		*Signed:*	
Approved by:		*Signed:*	

ACCIDENT / INCIDENT REPORT FORM

Incident Date:		*Reported by:*		*Report Date:*	
Incident Time:		*Location:*			

Person Involved /Injured:	Employee	Contractor	Visitor	General Public	Member	Other
Full Name:						
Address:						
Tel:			*Email:*			

DESCRIPTION OF ACCIDENT / INCIDENT

ACTION TAKEN / ACTIONS WHICH MAY PREVENT FUTURE REOCCURRENCE

WITNESS/ES

Full Name:		*Contact:*	
Full Name:		*Contact:*	
Full Name:		*Contact:*	
Form Completed by:		*Signed:*	
Approved by:		*Signed:*	

ACCIDENT / INCIDENT REPORT FORM

Incident Date:		*Reported by:*		*Report Date:*	
Incident Time:		*Location:*			

Person Involved /Injured:	Employee	Contractor	Visitor	General Public	Member	Other
Full Name:						
Address:						
Tel:			*Email:*			

DESCRIPTION OF ACCIDENT / INCIDENT

ACTION TAKEN / ACTIONS WHICH MAY PREVENT FUTURE REOCCURRENCE

WITNESS/ES

Full Name:		*Contact:*	
Full Name:		*Contact:*	
Full Name:		*Contact:*	
Form Completed by:		*Signed:*	
Approved by:		*Signed:*	

ACCIDENT / INCIDENT REPORT FORM

Incident Date:		*Reported by:*		*Report Date:*	
Incident Time:		*Location:*			

Person Involved /Injured:	Employee	Contractor	Visitor	General Public	Member	Other
Full Name:						
Address:						
Tel:			*Email:*			

DESCRIPTION OF ACCIDENT / INCIDENT

ACTION TAKEN / ACTIONS WHICH MAY PREVENT FUTURE REOCCURRENCE

WITNESS/ES

Full Name:		*Contact:*	
Full Name:		*Contact:*	
Full Name:		*Contact:*	
Form Completed by:		*Signed:*	
Approved by:		*Signed:*	

ACCIDENT / INCIDENT REPORT FORM

Incident Date:		*Reported by:*		*Report Date:*	
Incident Time:		*Location:*			

Person Involved /Injured:	Employee	Contractor	Visitor	General Public	Member	Other
Full Name:						
Address:						
Tel:			*Email:*			

DESCRIPTION OF ACCIDENT / INCIDENT

ACTION TAKEN / ACTIONS WHICH MAY PREVENT FUTURE REOCCURRENCE

WITNESS/ES

Full Name:		*Contact:*	
Full Name:		*Contact:*	
Full Name:		*Contact:*	
Form Completed by:		*Signed:*	
Approved by:		*Signed:*	

ACCIDENT / INCIDENT REPORT FORM

Incident Date:		*Reported by:*		*Report Date:*	
Incident Time:		*Location:*			

Person Involved /Injured:	Employee	Contractor	Visitor	General Public	Member	Other
Full Name:						
Address:						
Tel:			*Email:*			

DESCRIPTION OF ACCIDENT / INCIDENT

ACTION TAKEN / ACTIONS WHICH MAY PREVENT FUTURE REOCCURRENCE

WITNESS/ES

Full Name:		*Contact:*	
Full Name:		*Contact:*	
Full Name:		*Contact:*	
Form Completed by:		*Signed:*	
Approved by:		*Signed:*	

ACCIDENT / INCIDENT REPORT FORM

Incident Date:		*Reported by:*		*Report Date:*	
Incident Time:		*Location:*			

Person Involved /Injured:	Employee	Contractor	Visitor	General Public	Member	Other
Full Name:						
Address:						
Tel:			*Email:*			

DESCRIPTION OF ACCIDENT / INCIDENT

ACTION TAKEN / ACTIONS WHICH MAY PREVENT FUTURE REOCCURRENCE

WITNESS/ES

Full Name:		*Contact:*	
Full Name:		*Contact:*	
Full Name:		*Contact:*	
Form Completed by:		*Signed:*	
Approved by:		*Signed:*	

ACCIDENT / INCIDENT REPORT FORM

Incident Date:		*Reported by:*		*Report Date:*	
Incident Time:		*Location:*			

Person Involved /Injured:	Employee	Contractor	Visitor	General Public	Member	Other
Full Name:						
Address:						
Tel:			*Email:*			

DESCRIPTION OF ACCIDENT / INCIDENT

ACTION TAKEN / ACTIONS WHICH MAY PREVENT FUTURE REOCCURRENCE

WITNESS/ES

Full Name:		*Contact:*	
Full Name:		*Contact:*	
Full Name:		*Contact:*	
Form Completed by:		*Signed:*	
Approved by:		*Signed:*	

ACCIDENT / INCIDENT REPORT FORM

Incident Date:		*Reported by:*		*Report Date:*	
Incident Time:		*Location:*			

Person Involved /Injured:	Employee	Contractor	Visitor	General Public	Member	Other
Full Name:						
Address:						
Tel:			*Email:*			

DESCRIPTION OF ACCIDENT / INCIDENT

ACTION TAKEN / ACTIONS WHICH MAY PREVENT FUTURE REOCCURRENCE

WITNESS/ES

Full Name:		*Contact:*	
Full Name:		*Contact:*	
Full Name:		*Contact:*	
Form Completed by:		*Signed:*	
Approved by:		*Signed:*	

ACCIDENT / INCIDENT REPORT FORM

Incident Date:		*Reported by:*		*Report Date:*	
Incident Time:		*Location:*			

Person Involved /Injured:	Employee	Contractor	Visitor	General Public	Member	Other
Full Name:						
Address:						
Tel:			*Email:*			

DESCRIPTION OF ACCIDENT / INCIDENT

ACTION TAKEN / ACTIONS WHICH MAY PREVENT FUTURE REOCCURRENCE

WITNESS/ES

Full Name:		*Contact:*	
Full Name:		*Contact:*	
Full Name:		*Contact:*	
Form Completed by:		*Signed:*	
Approved by:		*Signed:*	

ACCIDENT / INCIDENT REPORT FORM

Incident Date:		*Reported by:*		*Report Date:*	
Incident Time:		*Location:*			

Person Involved /Injured:	Employee	Contractor	Visitor	General Public	Member	Other
Full Name:						
Address:						
Tel:			*Email:*			

DESCRIPTION OF ACCIDENT / INCIDENT

ACTION TAKEN / ACTIONS WHICH MAY PREVENT FUTURE REOCCURRENCE

WITNESS/ES

Full Name:		*Contact:*	
Full Name:		*Contact:*	
Full Name:		*Contact:*	
Form Completed by:		*Signed:*	
Approved by:		*Signed:*	

ACCIDENT / INCIDENT REPORT FORM

Incident Date:		*Reported by:*		*Report Date:*	
Incident Time:		*Location:*			

Person Involved /Injured:	Employee	Contractor	Visitor	General Public	Member	Other
Full Name:						
Address:						
Tel:			*Email:*			

DESCRIPTION OF ACCIDENT / INCIDENT

ACTION TAKEN / ACTIONS WHICH MAY PREVENT FUTURE REOCCURRENCE

WITNESS/ES

Full Name:		*Contact:*	
Full Name:		*Contact:*	
Full Name:		*Contact:*	
Form Completed by:		*Signed:*	
Approved by:		*Signed:*	

ACCIDENT / INCIDENT REPORT FORM

Incident Date:		*Reported by:*		*Report Date:*	
Incident Time:		*Location:*			

Person Involved /Injured:	Employee	Contractor	Visitor	General Public	Member	Other
Full Name:						
Address:						
Tel:			*Email:*			

DESCRIPTION OF ACCIDENT / INCIDENT

ACTION TAKEN / ACTIONS WHICH MAY PREVENT FUTURE REOCCURRENCE

WITNESS/ES

Full Name:		*Contact:*	
Full Name:		*Contact:*	
Full Name:		*Contact:*	
Form Completed by:		*Signed:*	
Approved by:		*Signed:*	

ACCIDENT / INCIDENT REPORT FORM

Incident Date:		*Reported by:*		*Report Date:*	
Incident Time:		*Location:*			

Person Involved /Injured:	Employee	Contractor	Visitor	General Public	Member	Other
Full Name:						
Address:						
Tel:			*Email:*			

DESCRIPTION OF ACCIDENT / INCIDENT

ACTION TAKEN / ACTIONS WHICH MAY PREVENT FUTURE REOCCURRENCE

WITNESS/ES

Full Name:		*Contact:*	
Full Name:		*Contact:*	
Full Name:		*Contact:*	
Form Completed by:		*Signed:*	
Approved by:		*Signed:*	

ACCIDENT / INCIDENT REPORT FORM

Incident Date:		*Reported by:*		*Report Date:*	
Incident Time:		*Location:*			

Person Involved /Injured:	Employee	Contractor	Visitor	General Public	Member	Other
Full Name:						
Address:						
Tel:			*Email:*			

DESCRIPTION OF ACCIDENT / INCIDENT

ACTION TAKEN / ACTIONS WHICH MAY PREVENT FUTURE REOCCURRENCE

WITNESS/ES

Full Name:		*Contact:*	
Full Name:		*Contact:*	
Full Name:		*Contact:*	
Form Completed by:		*Signed:*	
Approved by:		*Signed:*	

ACCIDENT / INCIDENT REPORT FORM						
Incident Date:		*Reported by:*			*Report Date:*	
Incident Time:		*Location:*				
Person Involved /Injured:	Employee	Contractor	Visitor	General Public	Member	Other
Full Name:						
Address:						
Tel:			*Email:*			

DESCRIPTION OF ACCIDENT / INCIDENT

ACTION TAKEN / ACTIONS WHICH MAY PREVENT FUTURE REOCCURRENCE

WITNESS/ES			
Full Name:		*Contact:*	
Full Name:		*Contact:*	
Full Name:		*Contact:*	
Form Completed by:		*Signed:*	
Approved by:		*Signed:*	

ACCIDENT / INCIDENT REPORT FORM

Incident Date:		*Reported by:*			*Report Date:*	
Incident Time:		*Location:*				
Person Involved /Injured:	Employee	Contractor	Visitor	General Public	Member	Other
Full Name:						
Address:						
Tel:			*Email:*			

DESCRIPTION OF ACCIDENT / INCIDENT

ACTION TAKEN / ACTIONS WHICH MAY PREVENT FUTURE REOCCURRENCE

WITNESS/ES

Full Name:		*Contact:*	
Full Name:		*Contact:*	
Full Name:		*Contact:*	
Form Completed by:		*Signed:*	
Approved by:		*Signed:*	

ACCIDENT / INCIDENT REPORT FORM

Incident Date:		*Reported by:*		*Report Date:*	
Incident Time:		*Location:*			

Person Involved /Injured:	Employee	Contractor	Visitor	General Public	Member	Other
Full Name:						
Address:						
Tel:			*Email:*			

DESCRIPTION OF ACCIDENT / INCIDENT

ACTION TAKEN / ACTIONS WHICH MAY PREVENT FUTURE REOCCURRENCE

WITNESS/ES

Full Name:		*Contact:*	
Full Name:		*Contact:*	
Full Name:		*Contact:*	
Form Completed by:		*Signed:*	
Approved by:		*Signed:*	

ACCIDENT / INCIDENT REPORT FORM

Incident Date:		*Reported by:*		*Report Date:*	
Incident Time:		*Location:*			

Person Involved /Injured:	Employee	Contractor	Visitor	General Public	Member	Other
Full Name:						
Address:						
Tel:			*Email:*			

DESCRIPTION OF ACCIDENT / INCIDENT

ACTION TAKEN / ACTIONS WHICH MAY PREVENT FUTURE REOCCURRENCE

WITNESS/ES

Full Name:		*Contact:*	
Full Name:		*Contact:*	
Full Name:		*Contact:*	
Form Completed by:		*Signed:*	
Approved by:		*Signed:*	

ACCIDENT / INCIDENT REPORT FORM

Incident Date:		*Reported by:*		*Report Date:*	
Incident Time:		*Location:*			

Person Involved /Injured:	Employee	Contractor	Visitor	General Public	Member	Other
Full Name:						
Address:						
Tel:			*Email:*			

DESCRIPTION OF ACCIDENT / INCIDENT

ACTION TAKEN / ACTIONS WHICH MAY PREVENT FUTURE REOCCURRENCE

WITNESS/ES

Full Name:		*Contact:*	
Full Name:		*Contact:*	
Full Name:		*Contact:*	
Form Completed by:		*Signed:*	
Approved by:		*Signed:*	

ACCIDENT / INCIDENT REPORT FORM

Incident Date:		*Reported by:*			*Report Date:*	
Incident Time:		*Location:*				
Person Involved /Injured:	Employee	Contractor	Visitor	General Public	Member	Other
Full Name:						
Address:						
Tel:			*Email:*			

DESCRIPTION OF ACCIDENT / INCIDENT

ACTION TAKEN / ACTIONS WHICH MAY PREVENT FUTURE REOCCURRENCE

WITNESS/ES

Full Name:		*Contact:*	
Full Name:		*Contact:*	
Full Name:		*Contact:*	
Form Completed by:		*Signed:*	
Approved by:		*Signed:*	

ACCIDENT / INCIDENT REPORT FORM

Incident Date:		*Reported by:*			*Report Date:*	
Incident Time:		*Location:*				

Person Involved /Injured:	Employee	Contractor	Visitor	General Public	Member	Other
Full Name:						
Address:						
Tel:			*Email:*			

DESCRIPTION OF ACCIDENT / INCIDENT

ACTION TAKEN / ACTIONS WHICH MAY PREVENT FUTURE REOCCURRENCE

WITNESS/ES

Full Name:		*Contact:*	
Full Name:		*Contact:*	
Full Name:		*Contact:*	
Form Completed by:		*Signed:*	
Approved by:		*Signed:*	

ACCIDENT / INCIDENT REPORT FORM

Incident Date:		*Reported by:*		*Report Date:*	
Incident Time:		*Location:*			

Person Involved /Injured:	Employee	Contractor	Visitor	General Public	Member	Other
Full Name:						
Address:						
Tel:			*Email:*			

DESCRIPTION OF ACCIDENT / INCIDENT

ACTION TAKEN / ACTIONS WHICH MAY PREVENT FUTURE REOCCURRENCE

WITNESS/ES

Full Name:		*Contact:*	
Full Name:		*Contact:*	
Full Name:		*Contact:*	
Form Completed by:		*Signed:*	
Approved by:		*Signed:*	

ACCIDENT / INCIDENT REPORT FORM

Incident Date:		*Reported by:*		*Report Date:*	
Incident Time:		*Location:*			

Person Involved /Injured:	Employee	Contractor	Visitor	General Public	Member	Other
Full Name:						
Address:						
Tel:			*Email:*			

DESCRIPTION OF ACCIDENT / INCIDENT

ACTION TAKEN / ACTIONS WHICH MAY PREVENT FUTURE REOCCURRENCE

WITNESS/ES

Full Name:		*Contact:*	
Full Name:		*Contact:*	
Full Name:		*Contact:*	
Form Completed by:		*Signed:*	
Approved by:		*Signed:*	

ACCIDENT / INCIDENT REPORT FORM

Incident Date:		*Reported by:*			*Report Date:*	
Incident Time:		*Location:*				
Person Involved /Injured:	Employee	Contractor	Visitor	General Public	Member	Other
Full Name:						
Address:						
Tel:			*Email:*			

DESCRIPTION OF ACCIDENT / INCIDENT

ACTION TAKEN / ACTIONS WHICH MAY PREVENT FUTURE REOCCURRENCE

WITNESS/ES

Full Name:		*Contact:*	
Full Name:		*Contact:*	
Full Name:		*Contact:*	
Form Completed by:		*Signed:*	
Approved by:		*Signed:*	

ACCIDENT / INCIDENT REPORT FORM					
Incident Date:		*Reported by:*		*Report Date:*	
Incident Time:		*Location:*			

Person Involved /Injured:	Employee	Contractor	Visitor	General Public	Member	Other
Full Name:						
Address:						
Tel:			*Email:*			

DESCRIPTION OF ACCIDENT / INCIDENT

ACTION TAKEN / ACTIONS WHICH MAY PREVENT FUTURE REOCCURRENCE

WITNESS/ES

Full Name:		*Contact:*	
Full Name:		*Contact:*	
Full Name:		*Contact:*	
Form Completed by:		*Signed:*	
Approved by:		*Signed:*	

ACCIDENT / INCIDENT REPORT FORM

Incident Date:		*Reported by:*			*Report Date:*	
Incident Time:		*Location:*				
Person Involved /Injured:	Employee	Contractor	Visitor	General Public	Member	Other
Full Name:						
Address:						
Tel:			*Email:*			

DESCRIPTION OF ACCIDENT / INCIDENT

ACTION TAKEN / ACTIONS WHICH MAY PREVENT FUTURE REOCCURRENCE

WITNESS/ES

Full Name:		*Contact:*	
Full Name:		*Contact:*	
Full Name:		*Contact:*	
Form Completed by:		*Signed:*	
Approved by:		*Signed:*	

ACCIDENT / INCIDENT REPORT FORM

Incident Date:		*Reported by:*		*Report Date:*	
Incident Time:		*Location:*			

Person Involved /Injured:	Employee	Contractor	Visitor	General Public	Member	Other
Full Name:						
Address:						
Tel:			*Email:*			

DESCRIPTION OF ACCIDENT / INCIDENT

ACTION TAKEN / ACTIONS WHICH MAY PREVENT FUTURE REOCCURRENCE

WITNESS/ES

Full Name:		*Contact:*	
Full Name:		*Contact:*	
Full Name:		*Contact:*	
Form Completed by:		*Signed:*	
Approved by:		*Signed:*	

Made in the USA
Las Vegas, NV
01 March 2024

86547445R00063